2nd Edition

The Hilario[us] Holiday Songbook

Contents

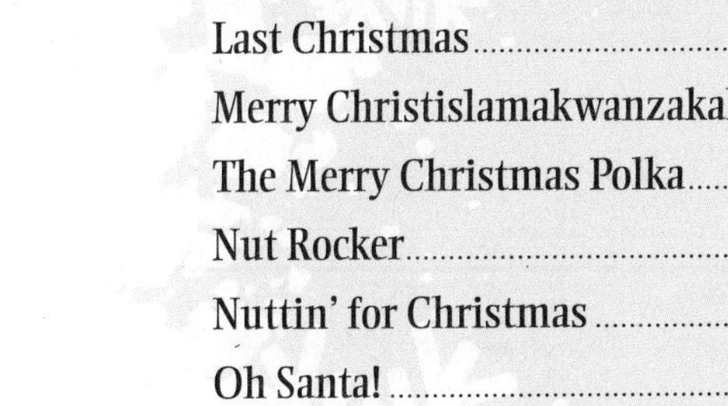

Alfred

Produced by
Alfred Music Publishing Co., Inc.
P.O. Box 10003
Van Nuys, CA 91410-0003
alfred.com

Printed in USA.

ISBN-10: 0-7390-8107-1
ISBN-13: 978-0-7390-8107-5

Cover Art
Burst: © iStockphoto.com / Aisle Think • Banner: © iStockphoto.com / urose • Snowflakes: © iStockphoto.com / K.J. Pargeter Images • Surprised Santa: © iStockphoto.com / Evrensel Baris Berkant

Alfred Cares. Contents printed on 100% recycled paper.

CHRISTMAS VACATION

(from *National Lampoon's Christmas Vacation*)

Words and Music by
BARRY MANN and CYNTHIA WEIL

Moderately ♩ = 88

C7
F
Ev - 'ry - bod - y knows there's not a bet - ter time of year.
Got our - selves the fin - est snow - man in the neigh - bor - hood.
Gm
Hear that sleigh? San - ta's on his way.
Ain't it fun, al - ways on the run?
B♭/C
F
Hip, hip, hoo - ray for Christ - mas va - ca - tion.
That's how it's done on Christ - mas va - ca - tion.
Chorus 1 & 2:
Gm
1. Got a ton of stuff to cel - e - brate.
2. Let's all deck the halls and light the lights.
(Bkgrd. both times) (Jing - a - ling - a - ling - a - ling - ling.

F
Now it's get - ting clos - er; I can't wait.
Get a toast - y fire burn - ing bright.
Lang - a - lang - a - lang - a - lang - lang.)
Gm
Gon - na make this hol - i - day as per - fect as can be.
Give Saint Nick the warm - est wel - come that he's ev - er had.
1.
F
Just wait and see this Christ - mas va - ca - tion.
We're so glad it's Christ - mas va - ca - tion.
2.
Bridge:
F
F/A
Gm7
G♯m7
And when the nights are peace - ful and se - rene,

Am7
B♭/C
we can cud-dle up and do our Christ-mas dream - ing.
F
Gm
(Bkgrd.) Jing - a - ling - a - ling - a - ling - ling.
F
Jang - a - lang - a - lang - a - lang - lang.
Gm

F
Christ - mas va - ca - tion.
Gm
B♭
Christ-mas va - ca - tion. Christ-mas va - ca - tion. Christ-mas va - ca - tion.
F/C
F
Gm
Christ-mas va - ca - tion. Christ-mas va - ca - tion. Christ-mas va - ca - tion.
F
We're so glad it's Christ - mas va - ca - tion.

Chorus 3, 4, (etc.):
Gm
1. Peace and joy and love are ev - 'ry - where.
2. 3. (etc.) Fa - la - la - la - la and ho ho ho.
(Bkgrd. all times) Jing - a - ling - a - ling - a - ling - ling.
F
You can feel the mag - ic in the air.
Jin - gle, jan - gle, jin - gle as we go.
Jang - a - lang - a - lang - a - lang - lang.
Gm
Let the spir - it of the sea - son car - ry us a - way.
F
Repeat ad lib. and fade
Hip, hip, hoo - ray for Christ - mas va - ca - tion.

CHRISTMAS WRAPPING

Written by
CHRIS BUTLER

Moderately ♩ = 112

Verse 1 (sing 1st time only):
A
1. Bah! hum-bug! No, that's too strong 'cause it is my fa - v'rite hol - i - day, but
Verse 2 (sing 2nd time only):
2. Cal-en-dar pic - ture, fro - zen land-scape chilled this room for twen-ty-four days.
D/A
C2
B2
all this year's been a bus - y blur. Don't think I have the en - er - gy to
Ev - er-greens, spar - kling snow, get this win-ter o - ver with! Flash - back to
A
add to my al - read-y mad rush just 'cause it's 'tis the sea - son. The
spring - time, saw him a - gain, would-'a been good to go for lunch,

D/A
C2
B2
per - fect gift for me would be com - ple - tions and con - nec - tions left from
could-n't a - gree we're both free. We tried, we said we'd keep in touch.
A
last year, ski shop, en - coun - ter, most in - t'rest - ing.
Did - n't, of course, 'til sum - mer - time, out to the beach to his boat, could I join him?
D/A
C2
B2
Had his num - ber but nev - er the time. Most of eight - y - one passed a - long those lines. So,
No, this time it was me, sun - burn in the third de - gree.

A
deck those halls, trim those trees, raise up cups of Christ-mas cheer.
Now the cal - en-dar's just one page, and of course, I am ex-cit - ed. To-
D/A
N.C.
I just need to catch_ my breath, Christ-mas by___ my - self___ this
night's the night, I've set my mind not to do too much_ a - bout___
A
year.
it.

1.
2.
D
G
D
G
D
G
1.
D
G
D
2.
D
G
F♯m
Em
Dmaj7/E
Chorus:
A
Mer - ry Christ-mas! Mer - ry Christ-mas! But I
think I'll miss this one this year. Mer - ry Christ-mas! Mer - ry Christ-mas! But I

1.
2.
think I'll miss this one this year. Mer - ry
think I'll miss this one this
Verse 3 (sing 1st time only):
A
3. Hard - ly dash - ing through the snow 'cause I bun - dled up too tight,
year.
Verse 4 (sing 2nd time only):
4. A. and P. has pro - vid - ed me with the world's small - est tur - key, al -
D/A
C2
B2
last min - ute have - to - do's, a few cards, a few calls be - cause it's
read - y in the ov - en, nice and hot. Oh, damn! Guess what I for - got? So

A
R. S. V. P. No thanks, no par - ty lights,_ it's
on with the boots, back out in the snow to the on - ly all - night gro - cer - y,___ when
D/A
C2
B2
Christ - mas Eve,_ gon - na re - lax,___ turned down all of my in - vites.
what to my won - der - ing eyes_ should ap - pear in the line is the guy I've been chas - ing all year!
A
Last fall I had a night to my - self, same guy called, Hal - low - een par - ty,
"Spend - ing this one a - lone,"_ he said, "Need a break, this year's been cra - zy." I

D/A
C2
B2
wait-ed all night for him to show,_ this time his car would-n't go.___ For -
said, "Me, too, but why are you..._ you mean you for - got___ cran - ber - ries too?"_ Then
A
get it, it's cold, it's get - ting late,__ trudge on home to cel - e - brate in a
sud - den - ly___ we laughed_ and laughed,_ caught on to what was hap - pen-ing,__ that
D/A
N.C.
qui - et way, un - wind, do - ing Christ - mas right__ this
Christ - mas mag - ic's brought this tale to a ver - y hap - py end -

A
time.
ing!
1.
2.
D
G
D
G
D
f

1.
G
D
G
D
2.
D
G
F♯m
Em
Dmaj7/E
Mer - ry
Chorus:
A
Christ-mas! Mer - ry Christ-mas! Could-n't miss this one this year! Mer - ry
Repeat and fade
Christ-mas! Mer - ry Christ-mas! Could-n't miss this one this year! Mer - ry

THE FRUITCAKE THAT ATE NEW JERSEY

Words and Music by
LAUREN MAYER

Em Bm/D G9 F♯7 Bm
in - no-cent sea - son is all the more rea - son to watch out or else you might meet. The
seethed and it churned 'til the ta - bles it turned; now it's eat - ing up peo - ple it - self! The
Chorus:
Em7 A7 D C♯m7(♭5) F♯7(♯9) Bm
fruit - cake that ate New Jer - sey nev - er shows an - y mer - cy de -
fruit - cake that ate New Jer - sey, it's caus - ing such con - tro - ver - sy.
fruit - cake that ate New Jer - sey, the darn thing's be - come so nerv - y. As the
C♯m7(♭5) F♯7 Bm C♯7 F♯7
vo - ur - ing ev - 'ry - thing in each town, and noth - ing and no one can slow it down.
Gob - bling up all of the Gar - den State, there'll be no es - cape if you hes - i - tate.
last crumbs of New - ark fall from its fork, next on its men - u is Old New York. With
Em7 A7 D C♯m7(♭5) F♯7(♯9) Bm
Ev - 'ry - one it would since meet, ends up as a hunk of mince - meat.
Ev - 'ry - one it would since meet, ends up as a hunk of mince - meat.
all of its vic - tims churned like de - bris on the Jer - sey Turn - pike.
A

To Coda
Em Bm G7 F♯7 Bm
hor - ri - ble fate, to end up on the plate of the fruit - cake that ate New Jer - sey!
1. G7 F♯7
2. G7 B
Bridge:
E
2. It
There's on - ly one fruit - cake on
B/D♯ C♯m7 C♯m/F♯ B C♯m7 F♯7
earth, I've thought, which we all give back and forth a lot. And ev - 'ry - one tells you the
D♯7 G♯7 C♯m11 F♯7 B Em7 A7
darn thing's got the tex - ture and taste of gran - ite! So think a - bout some - thing we

D
C♯m7(♭5)
F♯7
Bm
C7
Bm
may have missed; if no one eats fruit-cake on an - y list, then how has it man-aged to still ex - ist, if
C♯7
F♯7
G7
F♯7
D.S. 𝄋 al Coda
ev - 'ry - one tends to ban it? May - be it's from an - oth - er plan - et! The
Coda
F♯7
Bm
G7
Bm
rubato
fruit - cake that ate New Jer - sey. The mor - al of this tale of woe and hurt?
F♯m7(♭5)/C
F♯7
Slowly
Bm
F♯7
Bm
a tempo
Stick to the fruit cup, and skip des - sert!
a tempo

GET DRUNK AND MAKE OUT THIS CHRISTMAS

Words and Music by
DAN FINNERTY, JEREMY RUZUMNA
and DAVID WILDER

D A G
How else can I say "Hap - py Christ - mas" to
but I see all your sor - row through your po - lite
D
you?
smile.
My
Those
D A G Bm
pres - ents, I know, in the past have been lame,
sweat - ers and pant - ies I've bought you be - fore
D A G
but I'm not a good shop - per; I say it with
still have tags con - nect - ed deep down in your

D
shame.
drawer.
...end solo)
Chorus:
G
A
D
This year, please don't make me go shop - ping at the
G
A
mall. How 'bout we don't buy
D
A/C#
Bm
G
each oth - er pres-ents at all? Hey, why don't we both just get

To Coda
A
G
G
D/F♯
Em
D
drunk and make out this Christ - mas?
1.
2.
2. Yeah, I've
Bridge:
C
Em
Bm
I wan - na kiss you and hold you and touch you and tick - le your fan - cy 'til
C
Em/B
morn - ing. Now, ain't that bet - ter than some stu - pid gift card or pant - suit or

D/A
C
ear - rings or per - fume or Ugg boot or Swatch watch? I'll be ro - man - tic, light
Em
Bm
C
can - dles, get tan - tric, fill bath - tubs with flow - ers, talk feel - ings for hours.
Em/B
A
Then when it's time for some sex - y flir - ta - tion, we'll both get what we want; win -
D.S. 𝄋 al Coda
win sit - u - a - tion. Hap - py Christ - mas to

Coda
D
G
Yeah, why don't we both just get
A
G
G
D/F♯
Em
D
drunk and make out this Christ - mas?
(Spoken:) All to - geth - er now.
Slower, freely
G
A
Why don't we both just get drunk and make out this
rit.
G
G
D/F♯
Em
D
Christ - mas?

GOIN' ON A DATE WITH SANTA

Words and Music by
RANDY BROOKS

Am7 D7 Am7 D7
man with the big red bag. It's not a ro - mance, _ just
Am7 D7 G Am7 D7
din - ner and dance, _ but I know that tongues will wag. I'm
G
go - in' on a date with San - ta, I'm leav - ing my cares be -
E7 Am7 N.C. Am7 N.C. To Coda
hind, and I hope Mrs. _ Claus, I hope Mrs. _ Claus, I

Am7 D7 G E7 A7 D7
hope Mrs. Claus don't mind.
I
I'm
He
G D7
went to the mall and I sat on his lap, he gave me a pinch and I
roll-in' my hair up on lit-tle round pegs, I'm fluff-in' and gloss-in' and
knows that I'm naught-y, he says it's O. K. To tell you the truth, he pre-
G
gave him a slap. He hung can-dy canes from the front of my blouse; I
shav-in' my legs. I know that I'm sil-ly, I ought to get real; if he
fers it that way. I know he leaves gifts un-der ev-'ry-one's tree; but he
D7 N.C.
think some-thing stirred and it was-n't a mouse! He
sees when I'm sleep-in', then what's the big deal? He's
says that he's got some-thing spe-cial for me. I

D7 G D7
gave me a nod and I gave him a wink, he asked if I'd like to go
pick-in' me up a-round quar-ter to five, he says that we'll go to some
asked what she'd do if his wife ev-er found her jol-ly old man had been
G D7 G E7
out for a drink. I know that he's old and he's way o-ver-weight, but I
quaint lit-tle dive. I asked him which one and he said he's not sure, but it-'ll be
fool-in' a-round. He told me they keep their af-fairs to them-selves, and he'd
A7
1,2
D7
N.C.
3
D7
N.C.
D.S. al Coda
could-n't re-sist a ce-leb-ri-ty date. So I'm
some-place that does-n't mind rein-deer ma-nure. I'm
rath-er not talk a-bout her and the elves! I'm
CODA
Am7 D7 D7♭9 G G6/9
4 fr
hope Mrs. Claus don't mind.

GRANDMA GOT RUN OVER BY A REINDEER

Words and Music by
RANDY BROOKS

To Coda
B
E
D
A
as for me and Grand - pa, we be - lieve.
Verse:
E
B
1. She'd been drink - ing too much egg - nog
mp
E
and we begged her not to go,
E7
A
but she for - got her med - i - ca - tion, and she

B
E
stag - gered out the door in - to the snow.
C♯m
G♯m
When we found her Christ - mas morn - ing
B7
E
at the scene of the at - tack,
E7
A
she had hoof - prints on her fore - head, and in -

B
E
1st and 2nd time D.S.
3rd time D.S. al Coda
crim - i - nat - ing Claus marks on her back.
Coda
E
C#
F#
lieve.
Grand-ma got run o - ver by a
rein - deer
walk - ing home from our house Christ -mas
B
Eve.
You can say there's no such thing as

Verse 2:
Now we're all so proud of Grandpa,
He's been taking this so well.
See him in there watching football,
Drinking beer and playing cards with Cousin Mel.
It's not Christmas without Grandma.
All the family's dressed in black,
And we just can't help but wonder:
Should we open up her gifts or send them back?

(To Chorus:)

Verse 3:
Now the goose is on the table,
And the pudding made of fig,
And the blue and silver candles,
That would just have matched the hair in Grandma's wig.
I've warned all my friends and neighbors,
Better watch out for yourselves.
They should never give a license
To a man who drives a sleigh and plays with elves.

(To Chorus:)

GRANDPA'S GONNA SUE THE PANTS OFFA SANTA

Words and Music by
ELMO SHROPSHIRE, RITA ABRAMS
and JON GAUGER

Dm7♭5
G7
1
Cm
3 fr
2 Lively
C
world's most fa - mous case of hit - and - run.
One
make his loss much eas - i - er to
bear.
Grand-pa's gon - na sue the pants off - a San - ta,
G7
that's what Grand-pa's gon - na do.
Grand-pa's gon - na sue the pants
off - a San - ta 'cause Grand-ma would have want - ed him to.
C

Grand-pa's gon-na sue the pants off-a San-ta, he
knows the law is
thinks the law is
thought the law was
on his side.
G7
To Coda
Grand-pa's gon-na sue the pants off-a San-ta,
Cm
Ab/C
3fr
San-ta's go-in' for a ride.
F/C
Ab/C
Cm
Ab/C
Yes-ter-day the judge ar-raigned the
Now San-ta and the rein-deer wait the

F/C Ab/C Cm Ab/C Dm7b5 G7
rein - deer, Ru - dolph was the first to take the stand. They
ver - dict de - liv - ered by a jur - y of their peers:
Dm7b5 G7#5 G7 Dm7b5 G7
asked him for the truth a - bout ol' San - ta, Ru - dy said he's just a fat and jol - ly
six fat men with long and flow - ing whis - kers and half a doz - en pok - er - faced rein -
Cm Ab/C F/C Ab/C
man. (Spoken:) Now San - ta is be - fore the pro - se - cu - tion; he
dee. Now Grand - pa gets a T. V. for his suf - f'ring and
Cm Ab/C Dm7b5 G7 Dm7b5
looks a lit - tle thin - ner on the stand. (Sung:) And if they take a - way his fly - ing
San - ta is de - clar - ing bank - rupt - cy. (Spoken:) But lis - ten close - ly and you'll hear the

G7#5 G7 Dm7b5 G7
1 C
li-cense, there won't be an-y Christ-mas in the land.
law-yers (Sung:) sing-ing "Jin-gle Bells" as they col-lect their
2 C
D.S. al Coda
fees.
CODA
G7
San-ta's go-in' for a ride.
C G7 C
And Grand-pa's rid-ing by his side 'cause the
G7 C C6
law-yers took them for a ride.

GRANDMA'S KILLER FRUITCAKE

Two-Beat Country Swing

Words and Music by
ELMO SHROPSHIRE and RITA ABRAMS

C
F
grabbed the wife and chil - dren as the post - man wheeled it in; ___
C
___ a year - ly Christ - mas night - mare had
D7
G7
C
just come back a - gain. ___ It was hard - er than the head of
F
C
Un - cle Buck - y; heav - y as a ser - mon of Preach - er Luck - y;

C/B
Am
D7
one's e - nough to give the whole state of Ken - tuck - y a great big bel - ly
G7
C
ache! It was dens - er than a drove of barn - yard tur - keys;
F
C
tough - er than a truck - load of all - beef jerk - y;
To Coda
C/B
Am
D7
G7
dri - er than a drought in Al - bu - quer - que; Grand - ma's kill - er fruit -

C
cake!
C
Now I had to swal - low some
F
C
mar - gi - nal fare at our fam - 'ly feast I
D7
e - ven downed Aunt Dol - ly's pos - sum pie just to keep the fam - 'ly peace.

G7
C
— I winced at Wil - ma's giz - zard mousse, but
F
C
said it tast - ed fine. But that leth - al wea - pon
D7
G7
D.S. al Coda
Grand - ma baked is where I draw the line. — It was
CODA
C
A7
D
cake! It's ear - ly Christ - mas morn - in'; the

G
D
phone rings us a - wake. It's Grand - ma, Pa, she
E7
A7
wants to know... how we liked the cake? Well,
D
G
Grand-ma, I nev - er... we could-n't... it was un - be - liev - a - ble,
D
that's for sure! What's that you say? Oh, no Grand-ma, please! Don't

E7 A7 D
send us an - y - more! It was hard - er than the head of
G D
Un - cle Buck - y; heav - y as a ser - mon of Preach - er Luck - y;
D D/C# Bm E7
one's e - nough to give the whole state of Ken - tuck - y a great big bel - ly
A7 D
ache! It was dens - er than a drove of barn - yard tur - keys;

G D D/C#
tough - er than a truck - load of all - beef jerk - y; dri - er than a drought in
Bm E7 A7 1 D
Al - bu - quer - que; Grand - ma's kill - er fruit - cake! It was
kill - er fruit...
2 E7 A7 E7 A7
Man, that's kill - er fruit... Grand - ma's kill - er fruit -
D E7 A7 N.C. D
cake. Grand - ma's kill - er fruit - cake!

HEAT MISER

(from *The Year Without a Santa Claus*)

Words and Music by
JULES BASS and MAURY LAWS

B7 Em B7 Em
They call me Heat Mi - ser. What-ev - er I touch
Em7 A7 D7 N.C.
starts to melt_ in my clutch. I'm too much!
G
Refrain:
C
He's Mis - ter Green Christ - mas.
G Em G E7
He's Mis - ter Sun. He's Mis - ter Heat Blis - ter.

A7 D7 B7 Em
He's Mis - ter Hun-dred and One. They call me Heat Mi - ser.
B7 Em Em7
What - ev - er I touch starts to melt in my
A7 To Coda D7 N.C. G
clutch. He's too much! I
Bridge:
C7 B B♭
nev - er want to know a day that's un - der six - ty de - grees. I'd

A7
D7
rath - er have it eight - y, nine - ty, one hun - dred de - grees!
G
(Spoken:) Oh, some like it hot, but I like it REALLY hot! Hee hee!
D.S. 𝄋 al Coda
𝄌 Coda
D7
G
A♭7
G7
I'm too much. Too much!

I GUESS THERE AIN'T NO SANTA CLAUS

Words and Music by
BARRY MANILOW, JOHNNY MERCER
and EDDIE ARKIN

Moderate bluesy tempo (♩♩ played as ♩♪ in triplet (3))

A13 A7+ B♭13 A13 B♭13 A13
Jin-gle bells, wed-ding bells,
D9 G7 D♭9 C9
ring so mer-ri-ly, but jin-gle bells and
D♭9(♭13) C13 C7♭9(♭13) F6/9 Em7♭5 A7♯9(♭13)
wed-ding bells nev-er ring for me. Like the
Dm11 G13 Gm C7♭9 F B7♯9 E13♭9 E7♭9(♭13) A7♭13
clock on the shelf I hold hands with my-self. I guess there ain't no San-ta Claus.

Dm11 G13 Dm11 G13 Ebm11 Ab13
Ebm11 Ab13 Ebm11 Ab13 Ebm11 Ab13
I got wine, _ I got cheer. I got no - bod - y here. I
D.S. Instrumental solo
F13b9 Cb7 Bb+7 Ebm11 Ab13
guess there ain't no San - ta Claus. ___ Well, they
Ebm11 Ab13 Ebm11 Ab13
sure ___ got it right when they sing "Si - lent Night." I

Cm7♭5
F13♭9
F7♭9(♭13)
B♭13
B♭7♭13
guess there ain't no San - ta Claus.
Solo ends
C♭13
B♭13
C♭13
B♭13
E♭9
Lov - ers walk, hold - ing hands ev - 'ry where I go.
A♭7
D9
D♭9
D9♭13
A♭m9/D♭
D♭7♭9
Read - y, set, here I stand
G♭maj7
C♭13
Fm7♭5
C♭13
B♭13
E♭m11
A♭13
'neath the mis - tle - toe. Su - gar - plums in my head, on - ly

To Coda
A♭m7 D♭7♭9 G♭maj7 C7♯9 F13♭9 F7♭9(♭13) B♭7♭13
me in my bed. I guess there ain't no San - ta Claus
E♭m11 A♭13 A♭m7 D♭7sus D♭9/G G♭6/9 C♭maj7
My Dad and Moth-er told one an-oth - er
Cm7 F7♯5 B♭m9 Am9 A♭m9 D♭9
they saw a fu - ture for me. But since I've grown up
G♭maj7 C♭maj7 Cm7 C♭13 A♭maj7/B♭ B♭7♯9(♭13)
D.S. al Coda
I've got to own up: it's not like they said it would be.

CODA
F13♭9 F7♭9(♭13) B♭7♭13 E♭m11 C7♯9
guess there ain't no San - ta Claus. I
F13♭9 F7♭9(♭13) B♭7♭13 E♭m11 C7♯9
guess there ain't no San - ta Claus. I
Freely
F7♭9(♭13) B♭7♯9 E♭m11
guess, guess there ain't no San - ta Claus.

I'LL BE STONED FOR CHRISTMAS

Words and Music by
BOB RIVERS

B♭m7(4)
E♭7
A♭6
Christ - mas.
You can plan
Cm7(♭5)
F7
B♭m
F7
on me.
B♭m
D♭m
E♭
A♭
Cm/G
I must in - sist
on
the lem - on twist
Fm
A♭/E♭
Fm7(4)
B♭
F7sus
B♭
mar - tin - is
by the tree.

Eb7sus
Adim7
Bbm7
Eb7
Ab
Christ - mas Eve
G7(#9)
Bbm7(4)
Eb7
you'll find me
Ab6
Cm7(b5)
F7
Bbm
spark - in' up some green,
F7
Bbm
Dbm
roll - in' bones for

Ab Cm7(b5) F7 Bbm
Christ - mas din - ner, and sip - ping
Eb7 Ab Fm Bbm Eb7
I - rish cream. Oh yeah, that feels good now.
Ab G7(#9) Bbm7(4)
San - ta Claus will be fly - ing,
Eb7 Ab6 Cm7(b5) F7
whoa, stead-y now, with his rein - deer team.

B♭m
F7
B♭m
But I'll be crawl-in'
D♭m
A♭
Cm7(♭5)
F7
'round on the floor this Christ - mas, 'cause
B♭m
E♭7
Tempo I
A♭
E♭
some - one hid my keys.
molto rit., freely
a tempo
Fm
E♭
A♭
E♭7
A♭/E♭
E♭
A♭
(Spoken:) Oh, my. I think the keys are over here by the couch. What a lovely couch this is too. Is that naugahyde? Doesn't matter.
rit.

NUT ROCKER

By KIM FOWLEY

B7
Em
Am
D7
G
Am
D7
B7
Em
mf
B7
Em
Am
D7

G
f
8vb
8va
3
(8vb)
(8va)
15ma
loco
Gliss.
sfz

MERRY CHRISTISLAMAKWANZAKAH

Words and Music by
BRENT HARDESTY

Moderate two-beat (𝅗𝅥 = 88)

B♭
lit - i - c'lly cor - rect ac - tiv - i - ty. There's a catch - y lit - tle
E♭
Edim7
phrase, they say, that will cov - er ev - 'ry base, they say, and soon it will re -
B♭/F
Cm11
F7
B♭
B♭11
B♭7
place, they say, an - y greet - ings that of - fend. Mer - ry
cresc.
Chorus:
E♭
Christ - is - lam - a - kwan - za - kah, it's the per - fect hol - i - day
f

B♭7
greet - ing. Mer - ry Christ - is - lam - a - kwan - za - kah is a
E♭
wish that's worth re - peat - ing. No more San - ta hats or
A♭
Adim7
yar - mul - kes, no more "Deck the Halls" or "fa - la - la." Grab a hand, let's all sing
E♭/B♭
Cm
1.
Fm11
B♭7
E♭
F7sus
"Kum - ba - ya," Mer - ry Christ - is - lam - a - kwan - za - kah! Oh, it may
dim.

Verse 2:
Oh, it may sound a bit satirical,
It's so sensitive, it's so lyrical.
At the risk of sounding clerical,
It's an ecumenical miracle.
No more Santa Claus or evergreens,
No menorahs, dreidels, or manger scenes.
It's so theologic'lly squeaky clean
And it rolls right off the tongue.
(To Chorus:)

THE MERRY CHRISTMAS POLKA

Words and Music by
SONNY BURKE and PAUL FRANCIS WEBSTER

Moderately (Tempo di Polka)

Eb Bb F C F7
room we go. A - round and round the room we go, So get your - self a
Bb Bb
girl.
f
mf
F7 Eb Bb
Now ev - 'ry heart will start to tin - gle,
Eb Fdim F7 Bb
When sleigh bells jin - gle on San - ta's sleigh,
Bbdim F7 Eb Bb
To - geth - er we will greet Kris Krin - gle.

F7 Gb7 Cm7 F7 Bb7
And an - oth - er Christ - mas Day.
Brightly
Eb
Come on and dance The Mer - ry Christ - mas
dance The Mer - ry Christ - mas
mf–f
Ab
Pol - ka, Let ev - 'ry one be hap - py and
Pol - ka, Let ev - 'ry la - dy step with her
Eb Bb7 Eb7 Ab Bb7
gay, Oh! it's the time to be jol - ly and
beau A - round a tree to the ceil - ing with
Eb Cm Fm Gm Fm Am7-5
deck the halls with hol - ly, So let's have a jol - ly hol - i -
lots of time for steal - ing, Those kiss - es be - neath the mis - tle-

Bb7 F7-5 Bb7 Eb
day! Come on and dance The Mer - ry Christ - mas
toe! Come on and dance The Mer - ry Christ - mas
Ab
Pol - ka, An - oth - er joy - ous sea - son has be -
Pol - ka, With ev - 'ry bod - y join - ing in the
G G7 F#7 G7 Fm7 Bb7
gun, Roll out the yule - tide bar - rels and
fun, Roll out the bar - rels that cheer you and
Gm7 Cm Fm7 Bbdim Fm Eb Bb7
sing out the car - ols,
shout 'til they hear you, A Mer - ry Christ - mas ev - 'ry
Eb Bbdim Bb7 Eb Ab6 Eb
one! Come on and one!

LAST CHRISTMAS

Words and Music by
GEORGE MICHAEL

Moderately steady beat ♩ = 108

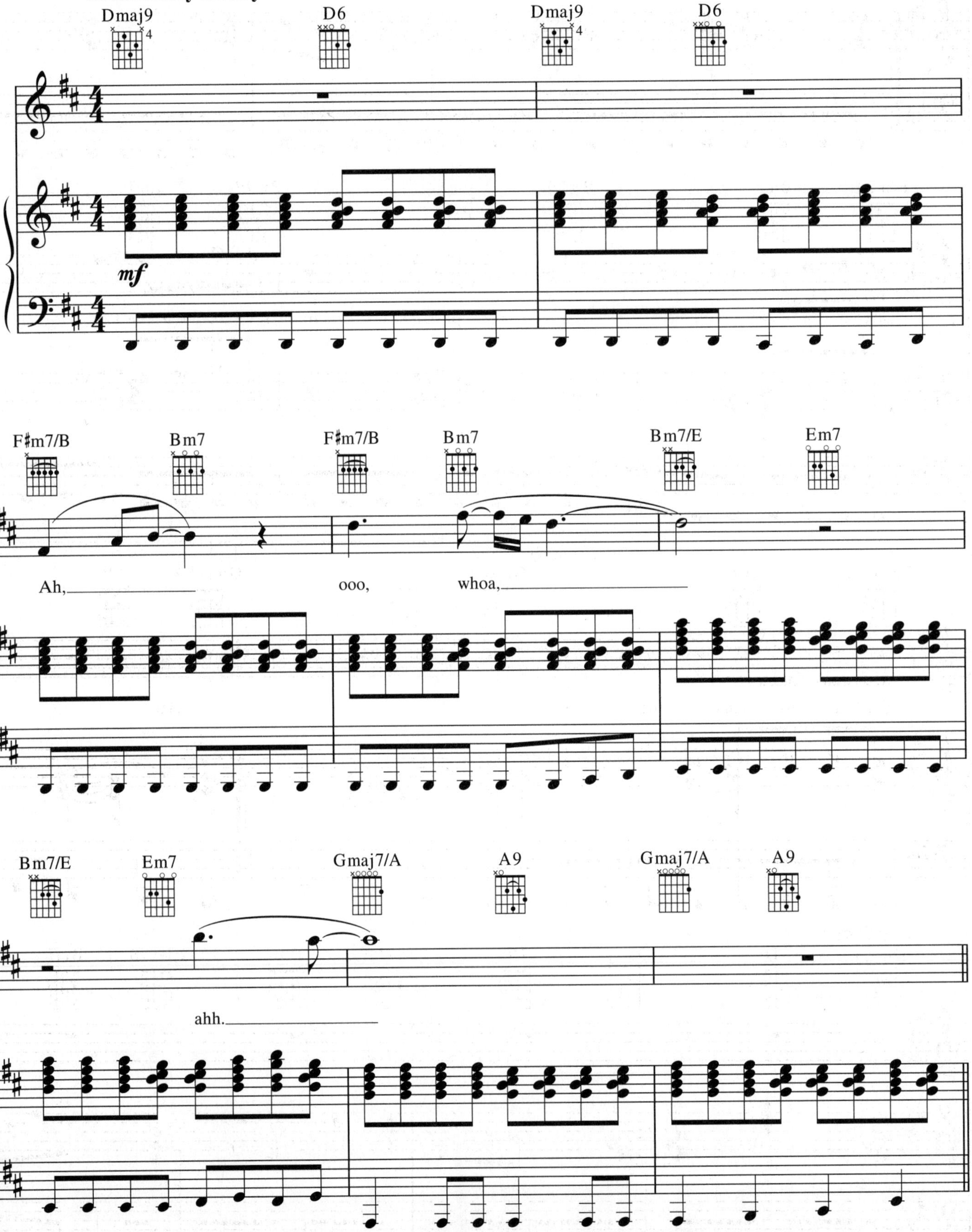

Chorus:
Dmaj9
D6
Dmaj9
D6
F♯m7/B
Bm7
Last Christ - mas I gave you my heart, but the ver - y next day you
F♯m7/B
Bm7
Bm7/E
Em7
Bm7/E
Em7
gave it a - way. This year to save me from tears I'll
To Coda
1.3.5.
2.4.
Gmaj7/A
A9
Gmaj7/A
A9
Gmaj7/A
A9
give it to some - one spe - cial. cial.
Interlude:
Dmaj9
D6
Dmaj9
D6
F♯m7/B
Bm7
F♯m7/B
Bm7

Em9
Em7
Em9
Em
Gmaj7/A
A9
Gmaj7/A
A7
Verse 1 (sing 1st time only):
Dmaj9
D6
Dmaj9
D6
F♯m7/B
Bm7
1.Once bit - ten and twice shy,
I keep my dis-tance but
Verse 2 (sing 2nd time only):
2. A crowd - ed room, friends with tired eyes,
I'm hid - ing from you
F♯m7/B
Bm7
Bm7/E
Em7
Bm7/E
Em7
tears still catch my eye.
Tell me, ba - by,
do you rec - og - nize me?
and your soul of ice.
My god, I thought you were
some-one to re - ly on.

Gmaj7/A A9 Gmaj7/A A9 Dmaj9 D6
Well, it's been a year. It does-n't sur-prise_ me. Hap-py Christ-mas, I
Me, I guess I was a shoul-der to cry__ on. A face on a lov-er with a
Dmaj9 D6 F♯m7/B Bm7 F♯m7/B Bm7
wrapped it up and sent it with a note say-ing, "I____ love you." I meant it.
fire in his heart,_ a man un-der-cov-er, but you tore me__ a -
Bm7/E Em7 Bm7/E Em7 Gmaj7/A A9
Now_ I know_ what a fool______ I've been._ But if you kissed me now,__ I know you'd
part.____ Ooo,__________ now I've found a real__ love. You'll nev - er

1.
D.S. 𝄋
2.
D.S. 𝄋 al Coda
(with repeat)
Gmaj7/A
A9
Gmaj7/A
A9
fool me a - gain.
fool me a - gain.
𝄌 Coda
Gmaj7/A
A7
Dmaj9
D6
Dmaj9
D6
cial. A face on a lov - er with a fire in his heart, a
F♯m7/B
Bm7
F♯m7/B
Bm7
Bm7/E
Em7
man un - der - cov - er, but you tore him a - part.
May - be next year

Bm7/E Em7 Gmaj7/A A9 Gmaj7/A A9
I'll give it to some - one, I'll give it to some - one spe -
Dmaj9 D6 Dmaj9 D6 F♯m7/B Bm7
cial, spe - cial. Some-one,
F♯m7/B Bm7 Bm7/E Em7 Bm7/E Em7
some-one. I'll
Gmaj7/A A9 Gmaj7/A A9
Repeat and fade
give it to some - one, I'll give it to some - one spe -

NUTTIN' FOR CHRISTMAS

Words and Music by
SID TEPPER and ROY C. BENNETT

B♭ F/A G7 C7 F B♭ F/A Gm
sis - ter's bed, some - bod - y snitched on me. I
Su - sie's hair, some - bod - y snitched on me. I
me be - cause some - bod - y snitched on me.
F F♯dim7 Gm7 G♭7 Gm7 C7(♭9)
spilled some ink on Mom - my's rug, I made Tom - my
did a dance on Mom - my's plants, climbed a tree and
Next year I'll be go - ing straight, next year I'll be
Fmaj7 Dm7 B♭ F/A B♭ Gm7
eat a bug. Bought some gum with a pen - ny slug,
tore my pants. Filled the sug - ar bowl with ants,
good, just wait. I'd start now, but it's too late,
C7/G C7 F6 C7(♯5)
Chorus:
F
some - bod - y snitched on me. Oh,
some - bod - y snitched on me. So,
some - bod - y snitched on me. Oh,
I'm get - tin'

Am/E
Dm7
F/C
nut - tin' for Christ - mas.
Gm
Gm/F
C7/E
Mom - my and Dad - dy are mad.
F
Am/E
I'm get - tin' nut - tin' for
Dm7
F/C
Gm
Christ - mas, 'cause I ain't been

C7(♭9)
1.2.
F6
Gm7
C7
nut - tin' but bad.
2. I
3. I
3.
F6
Gm
C
bad.
So you bet - ter be good, what -
F
D7
Gm7
C7
Am7
D7
ev - er you do, 'cause if you're bad, I'm warn - ing you,
Gm7
C7
F6
you'll get nut - tin' for Christ - mas.
rit.

OH SANTA!

Words and Music by
BRYAN COX, JERMAINE DUPRI
and MARIAH CAREY

Upbeat pop ♩ = 80

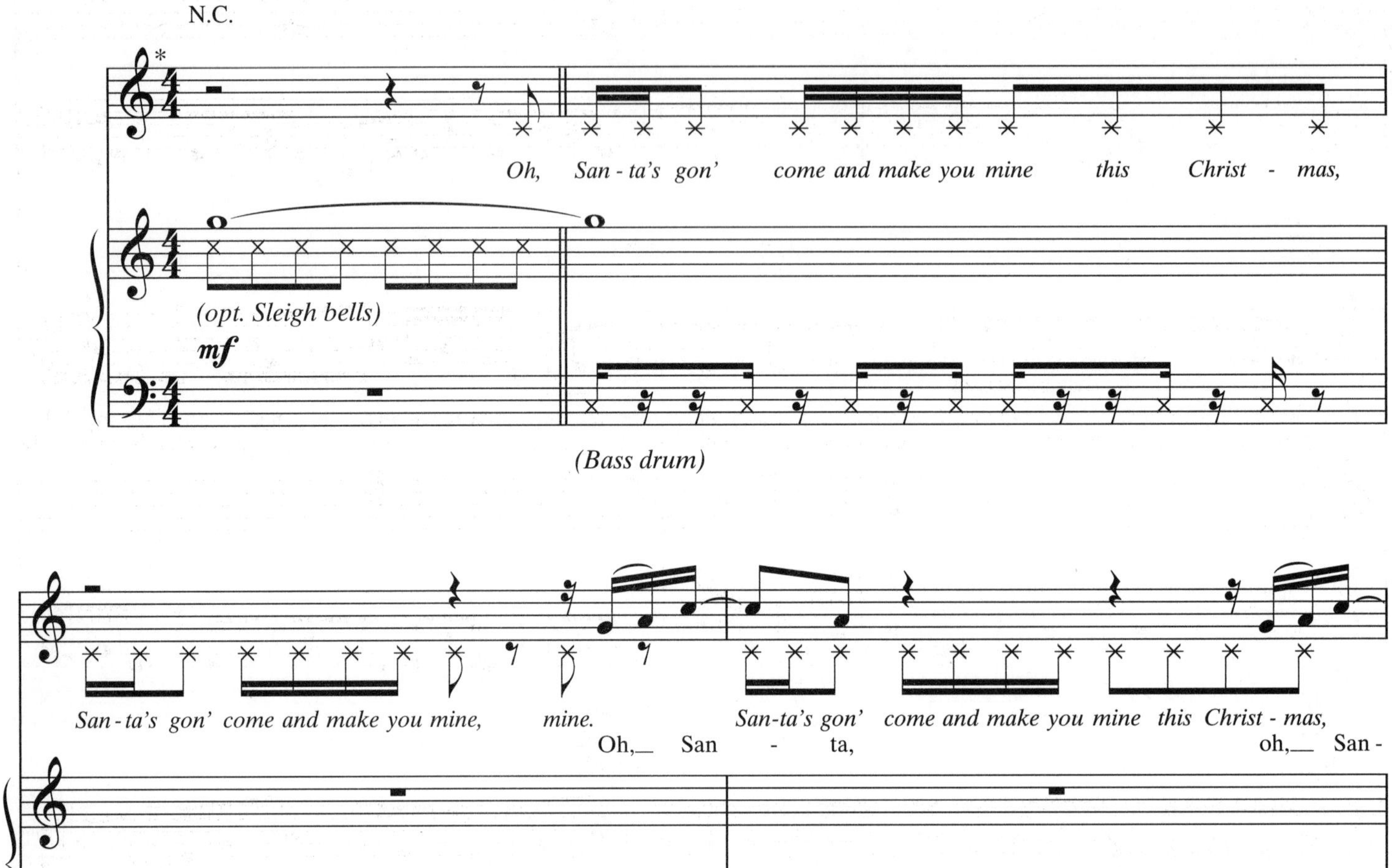

*Recorded in D♭ major.

G
F2
help me out? I know you're kind of bus - y with your elves right now. And I don't know how you
snow this year, so I hope Ru - dolph and them oth - er eight rein - deer get you safe - ly here, so
A♭
B♭
C
do the things you do while I sleep on Christ - mas Eve, but it's a - maz - ing, and I
you can scoop him up and scoop him right down my chim - ney. I've been real - ly, real - ly, real - ly
G
F2
bet that you could bring me back my ba - by, be - cause ev - 'ry time I see Christ - mas lights, I
good this year, so put on that red suit and make him ap - pear, 'cause Christ - mas cheer just
A♭
B♭
F
feel this burn in - side, and I just can't take it. I saw them shop - ping last week
ain't the same with - out my ba - by. Come on, oh, Kris Krin - gle, save me. They say it's un - real - is - tic,

Em7
Dm7
and his new girl was so bleak. And then I swore_ to my- self,
but I be - lieve in you, Saint Nick. So grant this__ wish for me right quick.
Chorus:
A♭
B♭
C
San - ta's gon - na come and make him mine this Christ - mas night.
Ho ho ho,
G
F2
San - ta's gon' come and make you mine this Christ-mas, San - ta's gon' come and make you mine, ho ho ho.
1.
A♭
B♭
San - ta's gon' come and make you mine this Christ-mas
2. Oh,
2.
A♭
B♭
San - ta's gon' come and make you mine this Christ-mas

Dm7
Em7
night.
Way oh, way oh, way oh.
Ooh,
Oh, San - ta.
Oh, San -
F
G
ooh, ooh, ooh, ooh,
oh, way oh, oh.
ta.
Oh, San - ta.
Oh, San -
Dm7
Em7
Way oh,
way oh, way oh.
Ooh
ta.
Oh, San - ta.
Santa gon' come and make you mine this Christmas.
Santa gon' come and make you mine, mine.
A♭
B♭
G
ah, ah, ah.
Oh, oh, oh. 3. Oh,
Santa gon' come and make you mine this Christmas.
Santa gon' come and make you mine, mine.

Verse 3:
C
G
San - ta Claus, if you get this let-ter, please don't make me wait. 'Cause all De-cem-ber, I'll be count-ing
F2
A♭
B♭
down the days, so hop on your sleigh. I prom-ise that I won't for-get the milk and cook - ies.
F
Em7
The trees are spar - kly and gold, but in - side, I feel so cold.
Dm7
A♭
B♭
So, soon as you leave the North Pole, San - ta, won't you come and make him mine this Christ - mas?

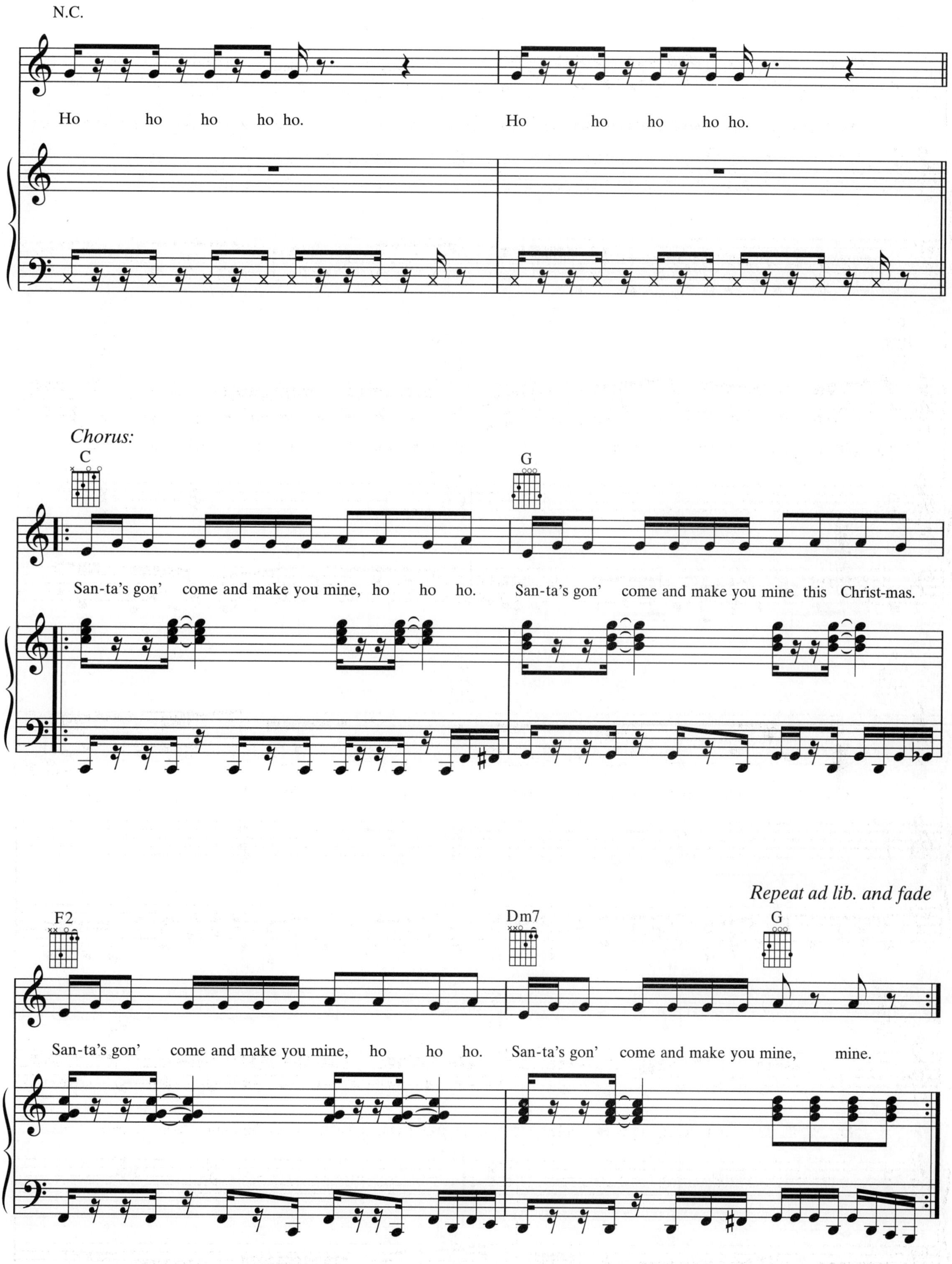
N.C.
Ho ho ho ho ho.
Ho ho ho ho ho.
Chorus:
C
G
San-ta's gon' come and make you mine, ho ho ho.
San-ta's gon' come and make you mine this Christ-mas.
Repeat ad lib. and fade
F2
Dm7
G
San-ta's gon' come and make you mine, ho ho ho.
San-ta's gon' come and make you mine, mine.

PLEASE DON'T BOMB NOBODY THIS CHRISTMAS

Words and Music by
DAN FINNERTY, JEREMY RUZUMNA
and DAVID WILDER

Slow gospel feel ♩. = 40 (♫ = ♩♪ triplet)

A/C♯
get it through to you to play nice with each oth - er? Don't
Bm7
A/C♯
D/E
make me sep - a - rate you; no more hat - er - at - in', sis - ters and broth - ers.
Amaj7
C♯7(♭9)
C♯7(♯9)
It seems like ev - 'ry - bod - y needs a lit - tle time - out. The
F♯m7
B9/D♯
bul - lies run - nin' loose, we're call - in' for a truce; a world full of doubt...

Dmaj7
A/C♯
grown - ups are ly - in' while ba - bies be cry - in'. We're
Bm7
A/C♯
D/E
all pick - in' sides, caus - in' di - vides, los - in' our pride. Here's all we're ask - in' you.
Chorus:
Amaj7
C♯7(♭9)
Please don't bomb no -
F♯m7
B9/D♯
bod - y this hol - i - day.
(Bkgrd.) Not on the hol - i - day.

Dmaj7
A/C♯
It just don't seem nice to bomb peo - ple. Don't fight: it's
Bm7
A/C♯
D/E
im - po-lite, it ___ ain't right, not to-night, not on the hol - i - day.
Bridge:
F♯m7
Em9
A7
In - stead of a bomb, ___ send a pear ___
Dmaj7
C♯7(♯9)
C♯7(♭9)
tree, or may - be a fruit - cake, or snow cone ma - chine. _

F♯m7
G13
Kill them with kind - ness and you'll un - der - stand,
D/E
you got to learn to use your frick - in' words in - stead of your hands.
Amaj7
C♯7(♭9)
1. (Spoken:) Come on, world;
2. Here's what I want you to do is dig deep down in your soul, and
F♯m7
B9/D♯
why you gotta bomb people,
especially on the holiday?
find some - one you can - not un - der - stand or frick - in' deal with at all.

Dmaj7
A/C♯
3
You bein' so naughty.
Yeah, maybe you need a big spankin'.
Go up and ask them to hang with you, walk in their shoe.
Bm7
A/C♯
D/E
3
The world needs a big, fat spankin',
and I'm gonna give it to you, a'ight?
Let me know how it go. I ain't walk-in' in no - bod - y's shoe. Shoes are nas - ty, ba - by.
(Nas - ty,
Bridge:
F♯m7
Em9
A7
All the world's_ prob - lems, they start out at home,_
ba - by.)
Dmaj7
C♯7(♯9)
C♯7(♭9)
_ so take care of all your bull - crap 'fore you walk out your

F♯m7
G13(♭5)
G13
door. Don't spread your hate germs and make us all
D/E
ill. Don't make me pull this world o - ver; you know that I will.
(Pull this world o - ver.)
Chorus:
Amaj7
C♯7(♭9)
Please don't bomb no -
F♯m7
B9/D♯
bod - y this hol - i - day.
(Bkgrd.) Not on the hol - i - day.

Bright gospel 𝅗𝅥 = 152
N.C.
(Spoken:) Don't bomb people, mother*******.
Keep it peaceful.
S***.
Am7
Please_ don't bomb, no.___ Please_ don't bomb, no.___
(Bkgrd.) Please don't bomb no - bod - y.
Repeat ad lib. and fade
Please_ don't bomb, no,___ not on the hol - i - day.___
Please don't bomb no - bod - y.

SANTA BABY

Words and Music by
JOAN JAVITS, PHILIP SPRINGER
and TONY SPRINGER

A7 D7 G Em A7 D7
slip a sa - ble un - der the tree for me. Been an aw - ful good girl,
lit - tle thing I real - ly do need; the deed to a plat - i - num mine,
G Em Am D7 G Em
San - ta Ba - by, so hur - ry down the chim - ney to - night.
San - ta hon - ey, so hur - ry down the chim - ney to - night.
Am7 D7 G Em A7 D7
San - ta Ba - by, a 'fif - ty - four con - vert - i - ble, too,
San - ta cut - ie, and fill my stock - ing with a du - plex
3
G Em A7 D7 G Em
light blue. I'll wait up for you, dear San - ta Ba - by, so
and cheques. Sign your X on the line, San - ta cut - ie, and

Am D7 G Em Am7 D7 G
hur - ry down the chim - ney to - night.
hur - ry down the chim - ney to - night.
B7 F♯m7/B B7 E7 Bm7
Think of all the fun I've missed. Think of all the fel - las that I
Come and trim my Christ - mas tree with some dec - o - ra - tions bought at
E7 A7 A9sus A7
have - n't kissed. Next year I could be just as good if
Tif - fa - ny. I real - ly do be - lieve in you. Let's
D Am7/D D7 G Em
you check off my Christ - mas list. San - ta Ba - by, I
see if you be - lieve in me. San - ta Ba - by, for -

A7 D7 G Em
want a yacht and real - ly that's not a lot.
got to men - tion one lit - tle thing, a ring!
A7 D7 G Em
Been an an - gel all year, San - ta Ba - by, so
I don't mean on the phone, San - ta Ba - by, so
Am D7 1. G Em
hur - ry down the chim - ney to - night.
hur - ry down the chim - ney to - night.
Am7 D7 2. G Em Am7 D7(♭9) G6/9

SNOW MISER

(from *The Year Without a Santa Claus*)

Words and Music by
JULES BASS and MAURY LAWS

B7
Em
B7
Em
Friends call me Snow Mi - ser. What - ev - er I touch
Em7
A7
D7
N.C.
turns to snow__ in my clutch. I'm too
G
much!
Refrain:
C
G
Em
He's Mis - ter White Christ - mas. He's Mis - ter Snow.

G
E7
A7
D7
He's Mis - ter I - ci - cle. He's Mis - ter Ten Be - low.
B7
Em
B7
Friends call me Snow Mi - ser. What - ev - er I
Em
Em7
A7
To Coda
touch turns to snow in my clutch.
D7
N.C.
G
He's too much! I

Bridge:
C7
B
B♭
never wanna know a day that's over forty degrees. I'd
A7
D7
rather have it thirty, twenty, ten, five, and let it freeze!
G
D.S. 𝄋 al Coda
𝄌 Coda
D7
G
A♭7
G7
Too much! Too much!
f

THE TWELVE DAYS AFTER CHRISTMAS

Words and Music by
FREDERICK SILVER

spite; Then with a sing - le car - - tridge, I
shot that blast - ed par - - tridge my true love, my
true love, my true love, gave to me.
f
The sec-ond day af-ter Christ-mas, I
mp

pulled on the old rub-ber gloves And ver - y gent - ly
mf
wrung the necks of both the tur - tle doves My
true love, my true love, my true love gave to
mf
me. The third day af - ter Christ-mas, my
f
mp

moth - er__ caught the croup; I had to use the
mf
three French hens to make some chick - en soup. The
four call- ing birds were a big mis - take, For their lang - uage was ob -
scene. The five gold_ rings were com - plete - ly fake and they

* *small notes are optional harmony parts*

My__ true love, my__
sev en of the swim - ming__ swans had drowned
My__ true love,
true love, my__ true love gave to me.
my__ true__ love, my true love gave to me.
rit.
mf
Slower (freely)
The eighth day af - ter__
Slower (freely)
rit.
mf
Christ-mas, be - fore they__ could sus - pect, I

Faster
bund - led up the eight maids a - milk - ing, Nine pip - ers pip - ing,
Faster
Ten lad - ies danc - ing, 'Lev - en lords a leap - ing, Twelve drum - mers drumming . . .
Spoken
Well actually I kept one of the :
broadly
Girls: drummers And sent them back col -
Boys: maids a - milking
broadly
ten.
lect. I wrote my true love, "We are through, love," And I

slight rit.
slightly faster
said in so— man-y words, "Fur-ther-more your Christ-mas gifts were
slight rit.
slightly faster
for the , birds!"
for the four— call - ing birds, Three French hens,
f
p
Two— tur-tle doves and a par - tridge— in a pear— tree.
mf
broaden
rit.
f
8

THE TWELVE PAINS OF CHRISTMAS

Words and Music by
BOB RIVERS, BRIAN SILVA
and DENNIS AMARO

Verse 2:
F/A
B♭
C7
F
sec - ond thing at Christ - mas that's such a pain to me:
C7
C7/B♭
F/A
D+
G9
C7
F
rig - ging up the lights, and___ find - ing a Christ - mas tree. 3. The
Verse 3:
F/A
B♭
C7
F
C7
third thing at Christ - mas that's such a pain to me: hang - o - vers,___
C7/B♭
F/A
D+
G9
C7
F
rig - ging up the lights, and___ find - ing a Christ - mas tree. 4. The

Verse 4:
F/A
B♭
C7
F
C7
fourth thing at Christ - mas that's such a pain to me: send - ing Christ - mas cards,
C7/B♭
F/A
D+
G9
C7
hang - o - vers, rig - ging up the lights, and find - ing a Christ - mas
F
Verse 5:
F/A
B♭
C7
F
tree. 5. The fifth thing at Christ - mas that's such a pain to me:
F/A
G7
C
C/B♭
F
F/A
five months of bills, send - ing Christ - mas cards,

F/A G7 C7 C7/B♭ F/A D+ G9 C7
hang - o - vers, rig - ging up the lights, and find - ing a Christ - mas
F Verse 6: F/A B♭ C7 F
tree. 6. The sixth thing at Christ - mas that's such a pain to me:
C7 C7/B♭ F/A G7 C C/B♭
fac - ing my in - laws, five months of bills, oh, I
F F/A B♭ F/A G7 C7 C7/B♭
hate those Christ - mas cards, hang - o - vers, rig - ging up these lights, and

F/A D+ G9 C7 F
Verse 7:
F/A
find - ing a Christ - mas tree. 7. The sev - enth thing at Christ - mas that's
B♭ C7 F C7 C7/B♭
such a pain to me: the Sal - va - tion Ar - my, fac - ing my in - laws,
F/A G7 C C/B♭ F F/A
five months of bills, send - ing Christ - mas cards, oh
B♭ F/A G7 C7 C7/B♭ F/A D+ G9 C7
geez, I'm try - in' to rig up these lights, and find - ing a Christ - mas

Verse 8:
F F/A B♭ C7 F
tree. 8. The eighth thing at Christ - mas that's such a pain to me: I
C7 C7/B♭
wan-na Trans-form-er for Christ-mas, char - i - ties, and whad-da - ya mean, your in - laws,
F/A G7 C C/B♭ F F/A
five months of bills, oh, mak-in' out these cards, ah,
B♭ F/A G7 C7 C7/B♭ F/A D+ G9 C7
E - dith, get me a beer, huh, what, we have no ex - ten-sion cords, and find - ing a Christ - mas

Verse 9:
F F/A B♭ C7 F
tree. 9. The ninth thing at Christ - mas that's such a pain to me:
C7
find - ing park - ing spac - es, Dad - dy, I want some can - dy, do - na - tions,
C7/B♭ F/A G7 C C/B♭
fac - ing my in - laws, five months of bills, writ - ing
F F/A B♭ F/A G7 C7 C7/B♭
out those Christ - mas cards, hang - o - vers, now why the hell are they blink - ing, and
3

F/A D+ G9 C7 F
Verse 10:
F/A
find - ing a Christ - mas tree. 10. The tenth thing at Christ - mas that's
B♭ C7 F C7
such a pain to me: bat - ter - ies not in - clud - ed, no park - ing spac - es,
C7/B♭
buy me some - thin', get a job, you bum, fac - ing my in - laws,
F/A G7 C C/B♭ F F/A
five months of bills, yo, ho, send - ing Christ - mas cards,

B♭ F/A G7 C7 C7/B♭ F/A D+ G9 C7
oh, geez, look at this, one light goes out, they all__ go out, and__ find - ing a Christ - mas
F
Verse 11:
F/A B♭ C7 F
tree. 11. The e - lev - enth thing at Christ - mas that's such a pain to me:
C7
3
stale T - V spe - cials, bat - ter - ies not in - clud - ed, no park - ing spac - es,
C7/B♭
Mom, I got - ta go to the bath - room, char - i - ties, she's a witch, I hate her,

F/A G7 C C/B♭ F F/A
five months of bills, oh, I don't e - ven know___ half these peo - ple, oh,
B♭ F/A G7 C7 C7/B♭ F/A D+ G9 C7
who's got the ter - let pa - per, huh, get a flash - light, I blew a fuse, and___ find - ing a Christ - mas
F
Verse 12:
F/A B♭ C7 F
tree. 12. The twelfth thing at Christ - mas that's such a pain to me:
C7
3
sing - ing Christ - mas car - ols, stale T - V spe - cials, bat - ter - ies not in - clud - ed,

no park - ing, waah, char - i - ties,
C7/B♭ F/A G7 C C/B♭
got - ta make 'em din - ner, five months of bills, I'm not send-ing 'em this year,
F F/A B♭ F/A G7 C7 C7/B♭
that's it, shut up, you, fine, you're so smart, you rig up the lights, and
F/A D+ G9 C7 F Fsus F
find - ing a Christ - mas tree.
rit.

THE TWELVE POUNDS OF CHRISTMAS

Words and Music by
TOM ZIGLER

C7 F C7
third pound of Christ-mas my moth-er said to me, You're big_ boned. I real-ly did-n't no-tice, and your
(Mother) (Male lead)
F B♭ F C7 F C7 F
butt still looks good_ to me. On the fourth pound of Christ - mas my grand-ma said to me, Are
(Female lead) (Grandma)
C7 F B♭ F C7
you re-tain-ing flu-id? You're big_ boned. I real-ly did-n't no-tice, and your butt still looks good_ to
(Mother) (Male lead)
F C7 G7
me. On the fifth pound of Christ - mas my friends all said to me, f The dry-er shrunk your
(Female lead) (All)

C7 F B♭ G7 C
jeans. mf You're re - tain - ing flu - id. You're big boned. I real - ly did - n't no - tice, and your
(Grandma) (Mother) (Male lead)
mf
F B♭ F C7 F C7 F
butt still looks good_ to me. On the sixth pound of Christ - mas my fa - ther said to me,
(Female lead)
C7 F G7 C F
Cut back just a lit - tle. f The dry - er shrunk your jeans! mf You're re - tain - ing flu - id.
(Father) (All) (Grandma)
f mf
B♭ G7 C F B♭ F C7 F
You're big boned. I real - ly did - n't no - tice, and your butt still looks good_ to me. On the
(Mother) (Male lead) (Female lead)

1st time: no repeat.
2nd time: play twice (for 8 and 7).
3rd time: play three times (for 9, 8, 7)
4th time: play four times (for 10, 9, 8, 7)
5th time: play five times (for 11, 10, 9, 8, 7)
6th time: play six times (for 12, 11, 10, 9, 8, 7)

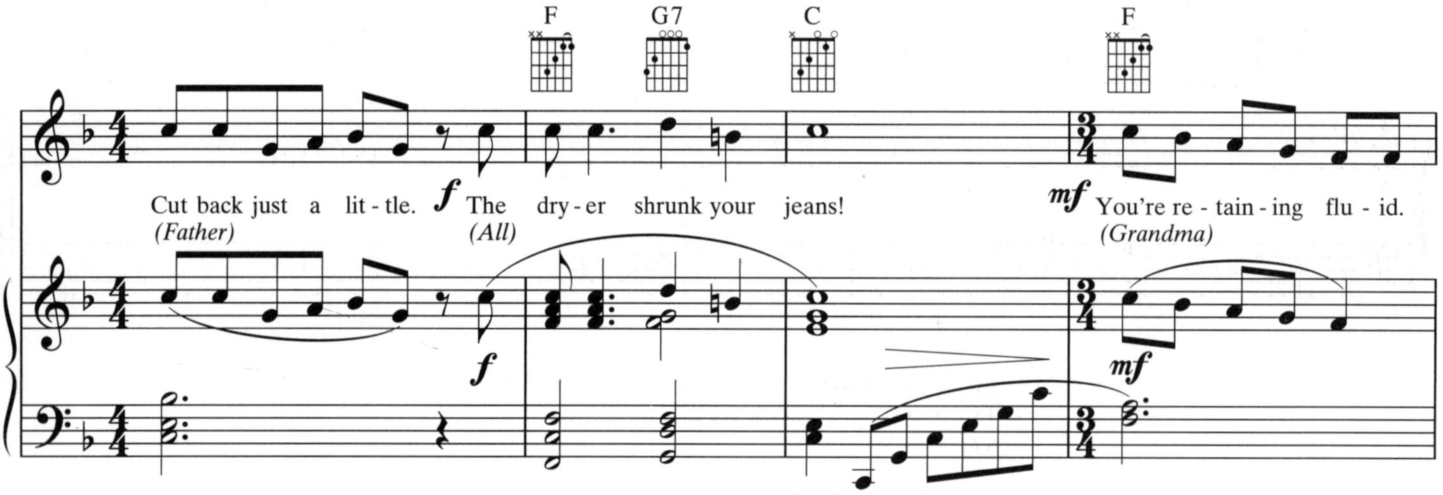

On the eighth pound of Christmas my sister said to me,
That's not on Weight Watchers. (etc.)
(Sister)

On the ninth pound of Christmas my cousin said to me,
I wouldn't wear that Spandex. (etc.)
(Female cousin)

On the tenth pound of Christmas my brother said to me,
Schedule liposuction. (etc.)
(Brother)

On the eleventh pound of Christmas my nephew said to me,
Grazing is for cattle. (etc.)
(Nephew)

On the twelfth pound of Christmas my mirror said to me,
Sooie, pig, sooie!
(Wicked Witch)

(Nephew)	Grazing is for cattle.
(Brother)	Schedule liposuction.
(Female cousin)	I wouldn't wear that Spandex.
(Sister)	That's not on Weight Watchers.
(Uncle)	Don't go back for seconds.
(Father)	Cut back just a little.
(All)	The dryer shrunk your jeans!
(Grandma)	You're retaining fluid.
(Mother)	You're big boned.
(Male lead)	I really didn't notice,
	And your butt still looks good to me.

WALKIN' 'ROUND IN WOMEN'S UNDERWEAR

Words and Music by
BOB RIVERS

C Eb7 Dm9 G7 Dm7 G7 G/D F/G
ted-dy with lit-tle straps like spa-ghet-ti. It holds me so tight, like
Em7 A7(b9 #5) D9 G7 C6
hand-cuffs at night. Walk-in' 'round in wom-en's un-der-wear.
Bridge:
Emaj7 F#m7 E/G# A Emaj7 F#m7 B7
In the of-fice, there's a guy named Mel-vin. He pre-tends that I am Mur-phy
Emaj7 Gmaj7 Am7 G E7(b9)
Brown. He'll say, "Are you read-y?" I'll say, "Whoa, man! Let's

Am9 D9 G11 A♭
wait un - til the wife is out of town." 2. Lat - er
Verse 2:
D♭maj7 D♭6 D♭ E7 E♭m9 A♭7
on, if you wan - na, we can dress like Ma -
E♭m7 A♭7 A♭ E♭m7 Fm7 B♭7(♭9 ♯5)
don - na. Put on some eye shade and join the pa - rade,
E♭9 A♭7 D♭6 A♭13 D♭maj7 D♭6
walk - in' 'round in wom - en's un - der - wear. Lac - y things,

D♭
E7
E♭m9
A♭7
E♭m7
A♭7
miss - ing; did - n't ask per - mis - sion.
A♭/E♭
G♭/A♭
Fm7
B♭7(♭9 ♯5)
E♭9
A♭7
Wear - ing her clothes, silk pant - y hose, walk - in' 'round in wom - en's un - der -
D♭6
B♭7(♭9 ♯5)
E♭9
A♭7
D♭maj9
B♭7(♭9 ♯5)
wear, walk - in' 'round in wom - en's un - der - wear,
E♭m9
Dm7(♭5)
D9(♭5)
D♭6/9
walk - in' 'round in wom - en's un - der - wear.

YOU'RE A MEAN ONE, MR. GRINCH

(from *How the Grinch Stole Christmas*)

Lyrics by
DR. SEUSS

Music by
ALBERT HAGUE

Verse 2:
You're a monster, Mr. Grinch!
Your heart's an empty hole.
Your brain is full of spiders,
You've got garlic in your soul, Mr. Grinch!
I wouldn't touch you with a
Thirty-nine-and-one-half-foot pole.

Verse 3:
You're a foul one, Mr. Grinch!
You're a nasty-wasty skunk!
Your heart is full of unwashed socks,
Your soul is full of gunk, Mr. Grinch!
The three words that best describe you
Are as follows and I quote:
Stink! - Stank! - Stunk!

Verse 4:
You're a vile one, Mr. Grinch!
You have termites in your smile.
You have all the tender sweetness
Of a seasick crocodile, Mr. Grinch!
(Spoken:) And given the choice between the two of you
I'd take the seasick crocodile.

Verse 5:
You're a rotter, Mr. Grinch!
You're the king of sinful sots.
Your heart's a dead tomato
Spotched with moldy, purple spots, Mr. Grinch…
(Spoken:) Your soul is an appalling dumpheap overflowing with the most disgraceful assortment of deplorable rubbish imaginable, mangled up in
…Tangled-up knots.

Verse 6:
You nauseate me, Mr. Grinch!
With a nauseous, super naus.
You're a crooked jerkey jockey
And you drive a crooked hoss, Mr. Grinch!
(Spoken:) You're a three-decker Sauerkraut and toadstool sandwich
…with arsenic sauce.

WIZARDS IN WINTER

(Instrumental)

Music by
PAUL O'NEILL and ROBERT KINKEL

Moderately fast ♩ = 144

Em Esus2 sus4 Em D/E G D/G G B Em B/E Em
B
Em Esus2 sus4 Em D/E G D/G G B
Em B/E Em B Em Esus2 sus4 Em D/E
G D/G G B Em B/E Em B

N.C.
f
Em
D/E
Em
D/E
Em
D/E
Em
D/E
Em
B
cresc.

Em
E sus2 sus4
Em
D/E
G
D/G
G
B
Em
B/E
Em
B
Em
E sus2 sus4
Em
D/E
G
D/G
G
B
Em
B/E
Em
B
dim.
8va
mp
loco
Em
mf

8va
(8va)
B
f
Em
Esus2 sus4
Em
D/E
G
D/G
G
B

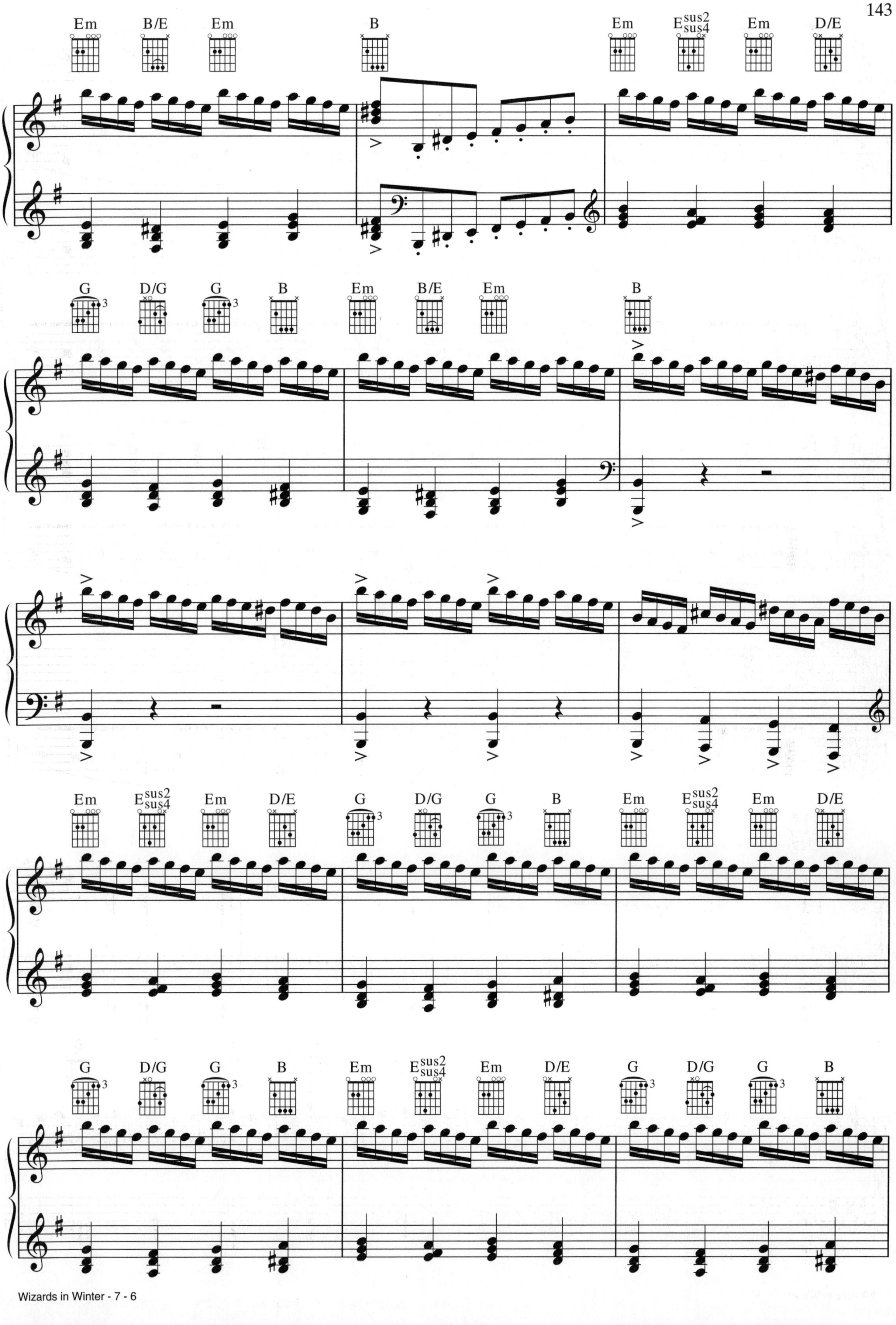
Em
B/E
Em
B
Em
Esus2 sus4
Em
D/E
G
D/G
G
B
Em
B/E
Em
B
Em
Esus2 sus4
Em
D/E
G
D/G
G
B
Em
Esus2 sus4
Em
D/E
G
D/G
G
B
Em
Esus2 sus4
Em
D/E
G
D/G
G
B

Em
D/F♯
G
D/A
Em
D/F♯
G
D/A
Em
G
Em
G
Em
G
Em
G
Em
cresc.
f
sfz